CRICKET ... DO IT THIS WAY

A certain four! M. P. Donnelly in action.

CRICKET . . .
DO IT THIS WAY

by G. A. WHEATLEY
and R. H. PARRY

With Photographs by
JOHN BARLEE, F.R.P.S.

and a Foreword by
M. P. DONNELLY

JOHN MURRAY, ALBEMARLE STREET, LONDON, W.

First Edition . . . 1948

Made and Printed in Great Britain by Butler & Tanner Ltd., Frome and London

CONTENTS

AUTHORS' PREFACE

This book has its genesis in another book entitled *Rugger—Do it this way*. Although dealing with different games, both volumes have the same object in view ; both originated in the precincts of the Royal Naval College, Dartmouth, and both have a common factor in the person of our untiring photographer, John Barlee, who during the past few months has taken, developed and printed no less than a thousand photographs. We feel, therefore, that we must first acknowledge our indebtedness to the authors of the Rugby book, and we shall be more than satisfied if we have maintained the high standard which they have set us.

In addition, our grateful thanks are due to Lt.-Cdr. Hodges, R.N., Lt.-Cdr. Marten, R.N., Lt. Crawley, R.N., Capt. Morriss, R.M., Mr. R. F. Thomas, Mr. R. A. R. Tonks, Cadet Plumer, R.N., Cadet Johnstone, R.N., Cadet Rivett-Carnac, R.N., and many other Cadets who helped in innumerable ways. Finally we wish to place on record our debt to Mr. Honeyman who, besides going to great trouble to prepare wickets for us, has given us the benefit of his knowledge and skill in the bowling section of the book. It goes without saying, however, that for any omissions or errors of judgment, we alone are responsible.

G. A. W.
R. H. P.

Dartmouth.
Sept. 1947.

Photographer's Note

Apart from those obtained from agencies, the photographs were taken at the Royal Naval College, Dartmouth. Readers may be interested to know that plates 25 and 73 are among the many that show Wheatley, and that Parry can be seen in action in plates 16, 53 and many others.

J. B.

FOREWORD

When first I picked up this small volume, I was greatly impressed by the title. It was simple and it was straightforward. It left no doubt what the book was about. Then, as I read through the chapters, I was charmed to find that these same admirable qualities persisted throughout the whole book—in its language, layout and its approach to the game it describes.

The authors have set out to teach people how to play cricket, and they have done well. There is much to praise. I like the liberal use of good photographs of great players ; photographs which give full weight to points explained clearly and without fuss in the narrative. I like the frank modesty of the writers. But most of all I applaud the emphasis which has been placed on the need for mastering the fundamentals of the game. The simple well-worn rules. Rules which we all know, but which we tend too often to forget, or even ignore. Such things, to mention but two, as watching the ball carefully all the time, and getting the head over and the foot to the ball, when making a stroke. In cricket, or in any game, it is impossible to overstress the importance of these fundamentals. All great players make the particular game they grace appear very easy to play, and they do so, I believe, largely by virtue of the careful and persistent attention which they pay to the basic principles of all ball games—concentration, footwork and practice. These three things are all-important, the latter especially. Rugger enthusiasts will be familiar with one of the golden rules for their game ; that of the three P's. For forwards—push, push and again push. For backs—position, possession and pace. I do not think that it would be amiss to say that the young cricketer, once he has grasped very firmly the importance of correct footwork, and once he knows how each shot ought to be executed, might well adhere to a similar rule. His three P's would be—practice, practice and still more practice.

A word or two about the authors. Garth Wheatley it was who held Oxford cricket together in the latter years of the war. Then, in 1946, he was awarded his " Blue " by D. H. Macindoe, for whose side he kept wicket with distinction. Garth must be ranked high among present-day keepers, and it is hoped that he will be able to turn out regularly for Surrey for years to come, and that he will continue to assist that county as ably as he did during the latter part of last season. As a batsman he will be the first to admit that he endeavours to sort out leg-breaks, top-spinners and googlies by a system that is peculiarly his own, and which to my mind smacks overmuch of the gambler. But there is a quality in his batting which might well be imitated more often than it is.   He has a fine scorn for the defensive method which uses the bat as a mere arrester of the ball's progress down the pitch, and given a half-volley or a long-hop, is quick to demonstrate to all that the bat, properly wielded, is an instrument of attack, a weapon by which the ball may be dispatched, without apology, but with great velocity, to the longest of long boundaries.

Ray Parry is a fine batsman whose style is eminently correct.   As a boy, he was given trials for Glamorgan, but the war interfered with his cricketing career.   Invalided out of the services, he played for Oxford in 1945, but recurrent ill-health has since prevented his taking his rightful place in " big " cricket.   He is now History master at the Royal Naval College, Dartmouth, and has there turned his talents to coaching Cadets.   There is no keener student of the theory and technique of cricket.   I have yet to decide whether he or Garth is the worse bowler !

Little need be said of John Barlee.   The technical excellence of his work speaks for itself.   Better known, perhaps, as a bird photographer, in this, and in other books in the same series, he has turned his attention to sport ; and the skill which enables him to stop a petrel in mid-air is here used to obtain action pictures of unsurpassed definition.

One last point : this book will, I feel sure, appeal to all followers of the game, and will be of assistance to all players.   But it will be of particular assistance to young cricketers, and to those who have the responsibility of instructing the younger generation, a task of very real importance in these post-war years when standards have to be rebuilt.

M. P. DONNELLY.

INTRODUCTION

THE purpose of this book is to teach the basic principles of cricket, as far as possible by means of visual illustration. Yet, because a certain amount of narrative and explanation is indispensable, this introduction will emphasise certain fundamentals which will be reiterated in the main sections of the book. Our chief aim throughout, however, is simplicity as far as this is consistent with the object in view.

THE FUNDAMENTALS

(a) Concentration

Of all the basic factors in cricket this is undoubtedly the most important, for it affects every phase of the game. Despite this, however, it is not sufficiently emphasised, with the result that it is too frequently forgotten. In part, at least, the genius of Bradman lies in his ability to exclude all else from his mind save the immediate task in hand. Concentration is absolutely indispensable. Notice that every time you are out, unless it is in some very unlucky manner, you will find on going over the incident carefully that you can remember *not* seeing the ball all the way. Probably everybody has heard the story that Bradman learned his cricket by first using a stump and a golf ball. This is said to have made keener his already wonderful eyesight. Whatever the truth of it, the point is that by some such method Bradman cultivated the habit of concentration.

Concentration is equally necessary to good bowling, although here, even more than in the case of batting, it must be allied with practice, of which more will be said later. You will observe in the section on bowling that stress is laid upon " length." Well, length is the product of practice and concentration. Say to yourself, as you run up to bowl, " I want to pitch the ball . . ." i.e. *will* the ball to go where you want it. Remember that the struggle between bowler and batsman is even more than the struggle of skill : it is in addition the struggle of wills.

No book on cricket can hope, adequately, to overcome the apparent prejudice existing among cricketers and others against giving fielding a place of equal importance alongside batting and bowling. All we can do here is to state categorically that many cricketers have failed to achieve fame because of weakness in this respect. Here, as elsewhere, *concentration* is of paramount importance. A good example to illustrate this occurred in a Test Match in Australia. Morris and Hassett had batted for hours. As

9

usual Hammond had fielded all this while at slip. He had hardly touched the ball all day. Suddenly, Wright spun one away quickly from the bat and Hammond took a sharp catch with his customary nonchalance. What had happened? Far from relaxing, Hammond had concentrated on every ball and his due reward had come after hours of mental exertion. Remember that in cricket a single catch can mean the difference between losing and winning a match. The fact that Yardley was dropped in the First Test Match at Nottingham in 1947 almost certainly cost South Africa the game.

When you look at the various sections of this book and consider the technique outlined in them, you should realise that you can achieve success only if you are prepared to concentrate. Like the taste for coffee, *concentration* is something which can be acquired. At first you may find it difficult, but persevere and you'll be surprised that it almost becomes a habit.

Rule 1, therefore, is: *concentrate on the ball.*

(b) Perseverance

The Need to Practise. This appears to be so obvious that it seems hardly worth mentioning. Yet the fact remains that one of the major weaknesses of English cricket after the war was simply lack of practice. During the years 1939–1945 relatively little first-class cricket was played in England, and this lack of practice in the game generally is only now being made up. It is true that a very small percentage of cricketers play well after only relatively little practice, but this does not affect the main point, for even the best cricketers usually need a few games before they run into their best form.

With practice a good cricketer can become great, an average cricketer can become good and a poor cricketer can become proficient. If you are keen enough to want to play a reasonable game you can do so by practising the technique illustrated in this book: you cannot do so merely by looking at the photographs and by doing nothing else. Remember too that practice means perseverance. Don't get downhearted and dismayed if you find that a stroke does not come easily to you or that it is difficult to get your feet in position at the right time. If you persevere, all will come right eventually and you will get great satisfaction as the ball streaks from the bat, or, if you are a bowler, when it breaks sharply and the bails fly off.

This need for practice and thus for perseverance is well illustrated in the batting photographs showing footwork. Only when you use your feet correctly can you hope to become a good batsman, and since footwork is mainly a question of practice the conclusion is obvious.

It follows from what has been said that practice is essential in all departments of the game. It is, however, particularly necessary in the development of good slow bowling, and so we are devoting here a paragraph to slow bowling for all those young people who are on the threshold of their cricketing careers. In the world of cricket to-day it is undeniably true that the general standard of leg-spin bowling is much lower than that of other types. You have all heard of the law of supply and demand. Well, it applies in cricket too. Every team likes to include at least one good slow bowler if it can, and thus slow bowlers are in demand. On the other hand, the natural instinct of most young cricket enthusiasts is to pick up a ball and to send it down the wicket as fast as they can. Hence slow bowlers are at a premium ; i.e. their services are wanted and they have a good chance of getting picked for representative sides. This is especially true of the slow leg spinners. Now, the important question to ask is : " Why are there so few leg break bowlers ? " The answer is simply this : It is because the bowling of *good length leg breaks* requires a skill which can only be acquired by hours of patient practice. It also requires a great deal of courage, because after much net practice the slow bowler will on occasion get hit to all corners of the ground and sometimes over them. To sum up. The art of slow bowling is the reward of labour and lots of it.

Rule 2 is therefore : PRACTISE, *practise and then practise some more.*

In conclusion we wish to issue a word of warning. The technique illustrated in this book is, we hope, theoretically sound in that it affords an adequate basis for learning the game. Yet in cricket, as in most other phases of life, success can only be judged by results. If, therefore, you find that your favourite stroke is theoretically incorrect and yet it brings you many runs without getting you out, then continue to use it. Cricket is a great game because it demands a judicious combination of individual skill and team work, and our aim in writing this book is certainly not to regiment the former by introducing a system which has to be adhered to rigidly. On the other hand, there exist certain basic principles which, by experience, have been found to produce the most satisfactory results, and it is these that we have endeavoured to illustrate in the following pages.

BATTING

CRICKET is primarily a struggle between a batsman and a bowler, and on the result of this struggle all matches depend. We want to consider briefly on what basic principles the issue will be decided.

A great batsman has written, " The main problem in bowling is to induce the batsman to play forward when he ought to play back and to play back when he ought to play forward." We may add to this, " The main problem in batting is to play the right stroke to the right ball." We shall return to the bowler's problem later. The batsman's problem clearly consists of two parts.

(i) A batsman must be able to play strokes correctly.
(ii) A batsman must be able to pick the right ball for each stroke.

It is with the first part of this problem that the batting section of this book is chiefly concerned.

Technique. There is only one way in which to learn to play strokes correctly and that is to *practise.* Study the photographs in this book and try to imitate them. Better, watch the great players in action yourselves and see how they do it. Play the shots in front of a mirror, or with a friend to point out mistakes, until you are sure that you are playing them correctly and until they *feel natural.* Then go to a net and persuade someone to bowl or throw a ball to the right length for each stroke until you can play it confidently. When there is at least one shot that you can play correctly to each type of ball, your technique is sound.

Judgment. The second part of the problem, picking the right ball, is again a matter of practice. The basic rule is *watch the ball.* The more closely you watch the ball, the sooner you will see where it is going to pitch. Watch it in the bowler's hand ; from his hand to the pitch ; from the pitch to the bat. *Watch the bowler's hand.* A knowledge of what he is trying to do will help you to decide what stroke to play.

Concentration. Finally, concentrate. Watch *every* ball and play it as well as you can. You can only get out once !

Playing an Innings. A wicket has fallen and it is your turn to bat. You are wearing your pads, and your bat and gloves are ready to hand—no last-minute rush for you. Walk to the wicket slowly to allow your eyes time to accustom themselves to the light, but make sure that you pass the previous batsman before he reaches the pavilion. Take guard and glance round the field to fix the position of the fielders in your mind. Take up your stance and concentrate.

For the first few overs you will be content just to stay in, finding the pace of the wicket and getting a sight of the ball. Even so, play your defensive shots firmly—too much " dead bat " play encourages the bowler—but only use your attacking strokes to really bad balls. In particular, do not cut or hook until you are seeing the ball well. These shots leave a very small margin of error. Anything of a length, or short, outside the off stump should be left alone. (Cover up well—you cannot be l.b.w. if your legs are outside the off stump.) Anything outside the leg stump should be four runs.

When you find that you are timing the ball, you can start to attack. This does not mean start to hit. Try to place your defensive shots out of the fielders' reach for a single ; use your cut and hook ; find the gaps in the field ; keep the bowler worried. Be particularly sure that your defence is sound. If you find difficulty with any bowler, play him carefully. The fielding side will not mind you scoring runs if you look like getting out. If one of your shots is not going well, stop playing it. The nets are the right place to practise.

Always call clearly and run fast. Apart from the immediate gain of runs scored, it disorganises the field if you continually turn twos into threes and threes into fours. Take a few quick singles. You will draw the fielders in and make it easier to pass them with your forcing shots. (To help this policy the non-striker must back up well—*he* should never be run out.)

If you follow some such plan of attack, you will always score fast and be a delight to watch ; but occasions arise when a special effort to score quickly is needed. If your eye is in, you can hit fours and sixes to your heart's content, but if you have only just come in the attempt may lead to disaster. Try instead for a single off every ball. Six runs an over is a hundred and twenty an hour— good going this !

When at last you are out, or, as you may think, given out, go without fuss. Nothing was ever gained by questioning an umpire's decision on or off the field.

1

2

3

4

" PRELIMINARIES "

1, 2. Grip

The hands are close together and near the top of the handle.
The left hand grips more tightly than the right.
The knuckles of the left hand point towards the bowler.

3, 4. Stance

The actual stance is largely a matter for individual preference, but whatever your stance you must *feel comfortable*. Make sure that
the left shoulder points at the bowler;
the ball can be seen with both eyes;
the feet are slightly apart;
the weight is equally distributed between the feet.
You must be well balanced and ready for movement in any direction.

"Balance is the essence of batting"

5

6

5. Backlift

The arms and wrists pick up the bat in line with the wickets.
The left hand is in control of the movement.
The head is kept still. (Compare Plate 4.)

6. Wrong

The bat has been lifted in the direction of slip, and will therefore come down across the line of the ball. The cause of this fault is usually that the right hand has done the work instead of the left.

" Play down the line "

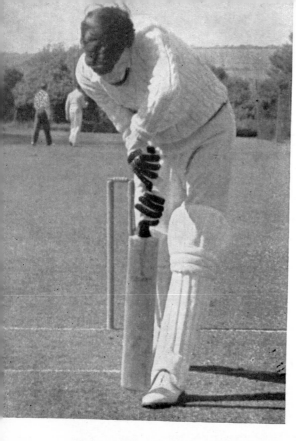

7

8

"THE FOUNDATION STROKE"

7, 8. Forward Defensive

The head is over the line of the ball.
The bat and left leg are close together.
The left elbow is up.
The right hand slips down to give greater control of the bat.

9. In Action

The right foot comes out to the pitch of the ball.
Note the position of the head, and the back lift.

A use of the wrists at the moment of impact often makes it possible to guide the ball past the fielders—particularly on the leg side, thus converting a purely defensive stroke into one of the most profitable in cricket.

"Get to the pitch of the ball"

10

11

10. Backward Defensive (i)

This is a purely defensive back shot which must be played with a dead bat. Note the following points :

the left wrist has been turned so that the bat can be kept vertical ;

the head and shoulders are right over the ball ; the right hand has slipped down the handle to give greater control.

Contrast the position of the batsman's body and feet with that shown in Plate 11.

11. Backward Defensive (ii)

In this form of back shot the ball can either be met with a dead bat or played firmly, depending on the bowler and the state of the wicket. The position of the body is similar to that for the forcing back shot (Plates 12 and 13), and indeed one shot can be converted into the other at the last moment by a use of the wrists. The following points should be noted :

the right foot moves back and over on to the line of the ball, remaining parallel to the line of the crease ;

the head and shoulders are over the ball ;

the bat is controlled with the left hand ;

in order to give free play to the wrists, the right hand does not slip down the handle.

"Watch the ball right on to the bat"

12

13

12. Forcing Back Shot (i)

The right foot moves back and across on to the line of the ball.

The eyes are on the ball.

Note the back lift—in line with the wickets.

13. Forcing Back Shot (ii)

The bat swings through with a pendulum movement, always in the line of the ball.

The left hand remains in control throughout the shot.

The swing of the shoulders gives power and freedom.

"Get Sideways"

14

14. Off Drive (i)

The eyes are on the ball.
The left foot comes out to the pitch of the ball.
Note the full back lift.

15. Off Drive (ii)

The weight is over the ball.
The ball is struck beside the left leg.

16. Off Drive (iii)

The eyes follow the ball.
Note the follow through. The left hand has remained in control and there is no sign of the right hand dragging the bat across the line of the ball.

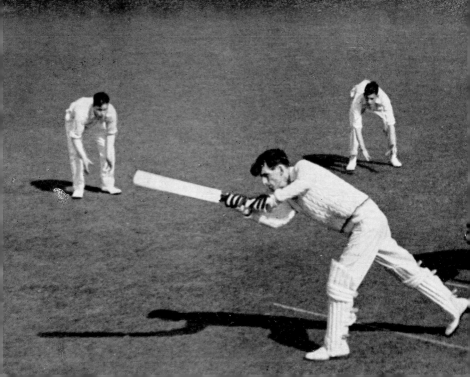

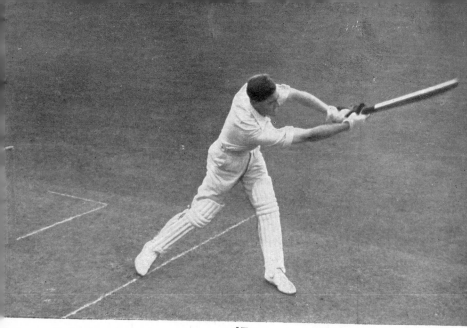

17

18

17, 18. Straight and On Drives.

The foot has come out to the pitch of the ball.
The bat has followed through along the line of the ball.
The ball is hit hard with a full swing.

The technique of these shots is similar to that of the off drive. The difference lies in the position of the left foot, which must in each case get to the pitch of the ball. Don't try to hit across the left leg.

On true wickets, against medium-paced bowling, both these shots can be safely used to loft the ball into the wide open spaces behind the bowler ; but—*swing down the line.*

"Keep the head down"

27

19

20

21

"LETTING THE BALL DO THE WORK"

19. Leg Glance (i)

The stroke is aimed at mid-on so that the full face of the bat meets the ball.

The right hand has slipped down to give greater control.

Note that the ball is being watched right on to the bat.

20. Leg Glance (ii)

The bat is turned at the moment of impact and the speed of the ball carries it down to fine leg.

21. Leg Glance (iii)

This shows the completion of the wrist movement.

The eyes are still on the ball.

"Aim at mid-on"

22

23

22. Chop Shot

The right foot moves across (not too far).

The right toe points in the direction in which the ball is to be hit.

The bat comes down on the ball with a chopping movement.

This shot must be played crisply.

23. Cut

The general position of the body and feet is very similar to that for the chop shot. The difference between the two strokes is that in the cut the wrists are brought into play at the moment of impact to give added speed to the ball.

Note the overlapping of the wrists which is clearly shown in this plate.

There is all the difference in the world between the genuine cut and a mere flash of the bat at the rising ball outside the off stump.

"Come down on the Ball"

24

24. Hook (i)

> The right foot moves back outside the line of the ball.
> The body faces the bowler.
> The left elbow is cocked and the left hand is still in control.

25. Hook (ii)

> The right hand and forearm force the bat through.

26. Hook (iii)

> The body and shoulders swing round, giving power to the shot.

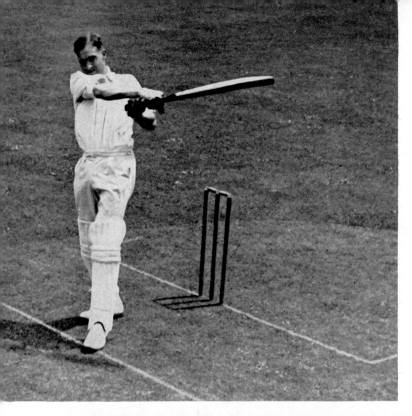

25

26

27

27. The Leg Hit

The right leg moves outside the line of the ball.
The body faces the bowler.
The whole weight of the body goes into the shot.

Aim the shot wide of mid-on. If you aim at long leg you will find that you will almost invariably be late.

The *Frontispiece* shows M. P. Donnelly at the finish of a leg hit. Note that his eyes are still following the ball. The full turn of the shoulders gives immense power.

" Hit it hard "

28. In

The batsman is running his bat in at the full stretch of his arm and will just make his ground.

29. Out

The umpire will have no difficulty over this decision ! Had the batsman grounded his bat it would have been a near thing.

When at the bowler's end, always *back up*. Besides being ready for a quick start, you can shorten the distance that you have to run by several yards (see Plate 49).

Call clearly and decisively. If in doubt say " wait."

" Run the first run hard "

28

29

BOWLING

We have said that cricket is primarily a struggle between batsman and bowler. How is the bowler to set about his task ? Let us first make a list of the chief reasons why a batsman gets out.

(i) Not looking at the ball
(ii) Playing a bad stroke
(iii) " The ball was unplayable "
(iv) Getting impatient
(v) Playing forward instead of back, or back instead of forward.

(i) and (ii) are clearly out of the bowler's control and (iii) we may leave to take care of itself. (iv) and (v) lie at the root of good bowling.

Length. The first necessity for any bowler is to be able to bowl a good length and to keep on doing it. Plain bowling to a length is known as bowling " tight," and its primary object is to keep the runs down ; but if you bowl to a length long enough, the batsman will become impatient and get himself out. All sides need at least one length or " stock " bowler. There is only one way to learn to bowl a good length and that is to *practise.* Go to a net with half a dozen balls, mark the spot where you think a good length ball should pitch, and bowl at it at your normal pace, without spin or swerve, until you can hit it regularly.

Variation. Plain length bowling will not get wickets quickly, and the next step is to make the batsman misjudge the ball. *Slight* changes of pace, without noticeable change of action, may make the batsman play the wrong shot. He may try to drive or hook a good length ball, or may play early or late ; but unless the ball is a good length, it will not (or should not) get a wicket. Therefore practise these slight variations in a net until you have them under control and *can still bowl a good length.*

Spin and Swerve. A good batsman who has misjudged a ball, can, by a use of his wrists, play it if it comes straight through. To be an attacking bowler it is therefore necessary to ally spin or swerve with length and variation of pace. But these latter must come first. A swinging long hop goes quickly off the bat and a half-volley has no time to spin. In a net practise spinning or swinging the ball, keeping a good length and introducing slight variations of pace.

Concentration. When bowling in a match, concentrate on every ball. One bad ball will give a batsman confidence ; several may put him right on top.

Leg Break Bowling. Leg break bowling requires such a pronounced finger and wrist movement that bowling to a length without spinning the ball is comparatively little practice. The prospective leg breaker may be well advised to learn to spin the ball first and to practise length second. But practise length he must.

Brainwork. " In the middle " the bowler has the help of nine fielders and a wicket-keeper, and the first rule of match bowling is *bowl to your field.* Decide on your plan of attack and, after consultation with your captain, place your field accordingly. Have in your mind a clear idea of how you intend to get each batsman out —two or three straight ones and then a quicker one outside the off stump for a catch in the slips, or whatever it may be. If at first you are unsuccessful, think of another plan and if necessary change your field. Do this unobtrusively ; do not advertise your intentions to the batsman. Sometimes you will find that you have to set different fields for two batsmen who are in together. Never be afraid to do this. It is a waste of a man to have a deep extra cover for a batsman who never drives.

Study each batsman carefully and try to find out his weak points. Is his back shot bad ? Keep the ball short of a length. Does he fancy his hook ? Feed him one or two easy ones and then another faster and farther up. Does he try to force the game ? Bowl him one or two steady overs and then a tempting one ; and so on. If you play several times against the same batsman you will come to know the best ways of getting him out. Think about the men to whom you will bowl to-morrow and work out a plan of campaign. *Always bowl with your head.*

Before you bowl each ball make sure that the fielders are in their places and that the batsman is ready. If the batsman continually has to stop you in the middle of your run up, it is your fault, not his. When the batsmen are running, do not just stand and look on. Get behind the wicket. There may be a chance of a run-out your end.

Finally, never be disheartened by a perfect wicket. It is then that your skill as a bowler will be tested to the uttermost. Respond to the challenge and call on all your stock of cunning to defeat the enemy.

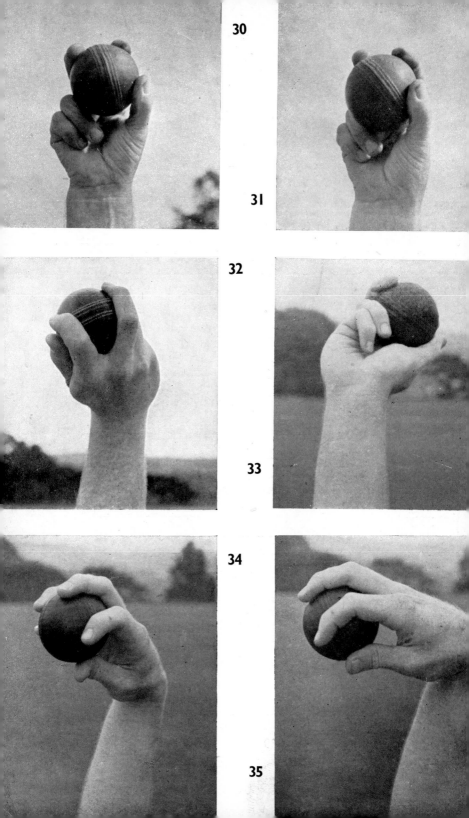

30

31

32

33

34

35

30. Grip for Away Swinger

The fingers are down the seam.
(Some bowlers have the thumb on the seam, under the ball.)

31. Grip for In-Swinger

The seam is held slightly across.
(Some bowlers have the first and second fingers close together and straight down the seam.)

32. Grip for Off Break

The fingers are round the seam.
Note the position of the forefinger, which can impart tremendous spin.

33. Off Break Delivery

The hand cuts under the ball.

34. Leg Break (side view)

The fingers are round the seam.
The hand comes over the ball, spinning it in the direction of gully.

35. Googly (side view)

The fingers are round the seam.
The wrist is turned and the ball is spun in the direction of long leg. (Compare Plate 34.)

36

37

36. Fast Bowling (i)

The left arm is raised.
The left foot is well up.
The whole body is " wound up " for a full swing.

37. Fast Bowling (ii)

The left arm is pulled down.
The left foot pounds into the ground.
The weight of the body swings forward.
Note that the body is sideways to the batsman and that the left foot goes straight down the wicket, not in the direction of slip.

38   39

38. Fast Bowling (iii)

As the ball is delivered, the right arm is straight and close to the head.

The whole body is taut and vertical.

39. Fast Bowling (iv)

The shoulders complete their swing.

A free follow through imparts life to the ball and gives a desirable feeling of aggression.

(The plates show Lieutenant-Commander J. Hodges, the Navy fast bowler.)

43

41

40

"AGGRESSION"

40. H. Larwood (Notts and England)

This shows clearly the beautiful rhythm of an almost perfect action.   Notice particularly the high position of both arms.

41. A. V. Bedser (Surrey and England)

Note the braced left leg, which forms a pivot for the swing of the body.

The eyes are still following the ball.

42. E. Toshack (New South Wales and Australia)

The right arm and leg are being used to increase the body swing.   Note the bowler's look of concentration.

42

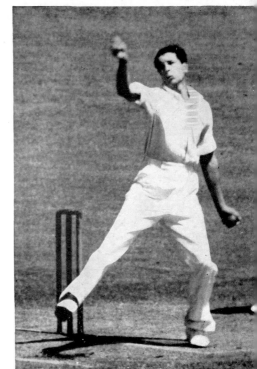

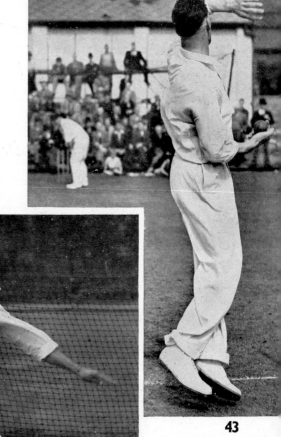

44

43

43. T. W. Goddard (Gloucester and England)

Note the left hand and arm ready to swing down, and the " sideways " position of the body.

The eyes are already fixed on the spot on which the ball will pitch.

44. T. W. Goddard (ii)

The left arm is doing its work, and the body is taut and beautifully balanced.

The right hand is ready to impart maximum spin to the ball.

In this plate Goddard is bowling round the wicket, an example which off spin bowlers are advised to follow on a sticky wicket. It gives a greater chance of an l.b.w. decision and the " one that goes straight through " may produce a catch in the slips. On a hard wicket, the decision whether to bowl over or round the wicket must be governed by the bowler's ability to spin the ball. Usually only the " master " can bowl " round " profitably under these conditions.

(For leg side field see Plate 47.)

" Accuracy comes first "

45

46

45, 46. D. V. P. Wright (Kent and England)

Again the same points are shown—the left arm—the sideways position—the balance of the body—the follow through.

Compare carefully the position of the right hand and wrist in the two plates, which shows the action for a leg break.

Leg spinners are not usually, indeed can hardly be expected to be, as accurate as other types of bowlers. This, however, is no reason why *you* should not assiduously practise bowling your spinners to a length. Always remember that a good batsman will " spot " most of your googlies and you can never rely on this ball alone to produce a record crop of wickets. Learn rather to flight your leg spinner and try to draw the batsman out of his ground. Remember that the wicket-keeper is your chief ally.

The basic field for a leg spinner is shown in Plate 49. You have two more men at your disposal. They will probably go in the outfield—the exact position depends on the pet shots of the batsman.

"Flight gets the wickets that spin can't"

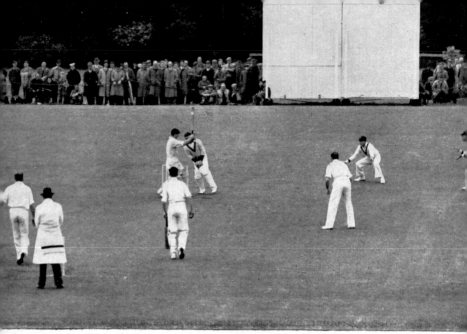

47

47. A. Rowan's (South Africa) Leg Trap

This plate shows the leg trap positions for one of the legitimate forms of leg theory. The bowler is bowling off spinners, hoping that the ball will be cocked up to one of the short legs or snicked to leg slip. If you want fielders to take up these positions when you are bowling you must cultivate accuracy.

In this plate it looks as though Rowan has slipped from his usually high standards !

The positioning of the three (or at most four) men available for the off side depends chiefly on the idiosyncrasies of the batsman.

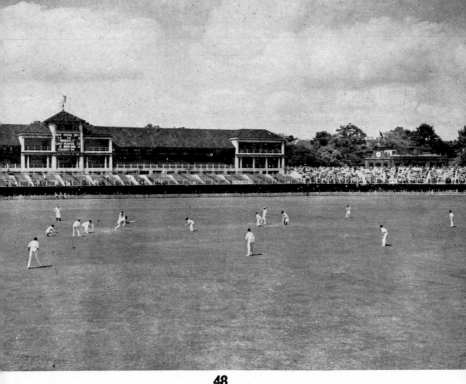

48

48. Field Set for A. H. Kardar (Oxford and India)

This plate shows an agressive field for a slow medium left-handed bowler. Such a field will normally be possible only on a sticky wicket. If the batsmen are attacking, silly point and second slip will be replaced by a deep extra cover and a deep long on.

Plates 49 and 50 show further examples of field placing. Plate 50 shows the close fielders for a fast medium swing bowler. Some bowlers would favour an extra slip or short leg, depending on the method of attack (out-swing or in-swing) that they were employing. Plate 49 shows the ordinary defensive field for a slow bowler. Two men, not shown in the plate, are available for the deep field positions.

FIELDING

In the struggle between the batsman and the bowler, the fielders are the allies of the bowler. They should take part in any plots hatched to trap the unwary batsman. The good captain will say, " Short leg, Jim ; they're lifting a bit and I hope you'll be able to pick up a catch," rather than simply " You take short leg." The bowler is helpless without his fielders, and they should be made to realise that he is relying on them. Few matches have been played in which a sharp chance taken or a " sitter " missed have not affected the result.

Position. A good fielder will generally have a position in which he is a specialist, and will field there most of the time ; but never forget that, at need, he must be able to field anywhere. A slip fielder may have to go deep, if only for a single over, and while there he may get a vital catch. He should be able to take it.

Learning to Field. Fielding, more than any other department of the game, can be learnt ; and it is learnt by *practice*. There is no excuse in cricket for bad fielding. Two keen cricketers, given a ball and any open ground, can and will learn to field. No equipment, no net, no prepared wicket is required. If you are a bad fielder, do not expect to be picked for any representative side, be it school, university, county or country.

Throwing. For some reason, never satisfactorily explained, England usually falls below other countries in the standard of the throwing. You may not be able to throw far, but by practice you can and should learn to throw quickly and accurately.

Concentration. It is more difficult to concentrate when fielding than when batting or bowling as you do not have so much to do ; but it is equally important. The quick start may save a single. The chance taken may win a match. If you can stay alert for a whole day, with perhaps only a dozen balls to field, and hold a sharp catch at the end of it, you are a good fielder.

In the Field. Apart from ability to stop and catch a ball, there are many points that go to make up a good fielder. First and foremost is the rule *always try for the catch*. You may be fielding on the boundary and the ball may be coming to you first bounce, so that it can be fielded easily. You should run in and try to make it into a catch. Never mind if, by so doing, you altogether fail to stop it. The crowd may say " Oooo . . . ! " but cricketers will realise what you have tried to do and applaud you. A chance of a wicket is always worth four runs. Similarly, if the batsman is out of his ground, throw hard at the wicket. Do not worry about possible overthrows.

As a general rule, throw in to the wicket-keeper, unless there is definitely a better chance of a run-out at the other end. He is wearing gloves, and is more likely to gather the ball cleanly than the bowler. When returning the ball to the bowler, lob him an easy catch. Do not make him bend, or risk hurting his hands with a hard throw (unless there is a chance of a wicket). Mid-off and mid-on should save the bowler trouble by picking the ball up for him and fielding as many of the straight ones as they can.

Save the wicket-keeper trouble. (This is a point often forgotten.) He works harder than anyone else in the field and should not be made to run or bend unnecessarily. Do not plug the ball at him as hard as you can, when there is no need for it. Hands can get bruised even through gloves, and the wicket-keeper's hands have quite a lot to stand up to in the course of a season.

Always be ready to back up. Back up other fielders when the ball is hit hard. Back up the bowler or the wicket-keeper when the batsmen are running and there may be a hard throw in. When backing up, leave yourself plenty of room. You should be at least twenty yards from the man you are covering. Otherwise he will unsight you and you may miss the ball as well.

Be on the alert, concentrate, and field as well as you can, and you will find that fielding is not mere drudgery; it is one of the most enjoyable parts of cricket.

"CONCENTRATION"

49. The Out Fielders

The field is set for a slow right-hand bowler. (Deep extra-cover and deep long-on do not appear in the plate.)

All the fielders, except slip, are moving in as the bowler bowls. If you are already on the move, you make a quick start in any direction.

50. The Close Fielders

The field is set for a fast medium bowler.
Note the concentration with which the fielders are watching the ball and the general air of alertness.

"Good fielding wins matches"

51

52

53

51. Slip Catch (i)

The fielder's whole attention is concentrated on the ball.
The hands form a cup to receive the ball.
The hands are away from the body, ready to give.

52. Slip Catch (ii)

As the ball is caught the hands give and the ball is drawn safely in to the body.
Note that the eyes are still on the ball.

53. Wrong

The fingers are pointing at the ball. This is both dangerous and incorrect.
The ball will strike the hard part of the hand and will probably bounce out.

"Get both hands to the ball"

54

55

"A SHARP CHANCE"

54. One-Handed

Here the fielder cannot get both hands to the ball.

The fingers of the right hand are extended and the hand forms a cup.

The left arm is used to preserve balance.

Note the look of concentration and determination that even the hardest chance will be snapped up.

55. A High One

Again—balance, concentration, determination.

"Watch the ball into your hand"

56

57

56. Right

The hands are cupped to receive the ball.

The ball is caught high up and, as the hands give, will be drawn in to the chest.

57. Wrong

The ball will be caught (or more probably dropped) too low and too far from the body.

In this position it is impossible to watch the ball right into the hands.

When fielding in the deep, always try for the catch. Do not hesitate because you may make the ball more difficult to field. A chance of a wicket is worth four runs given away.

A good deep fielder may make as much as twenty yards to the ball.

" Always try for the catch "

58

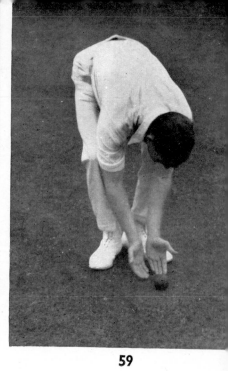

59

60

"ALONG THE GROUND"

58. Straight to Him

The fielder is moving in to the ball to prevent any chance of the batsman stealing a second run.

59. A Hard One

The ball is travelling fast and the feet are used as a second line of defence.

Note the position of the hands.

60. Saving the Single

Here the emphasis is on speed of return.

The ball is gathered with both hands for safety, while the weight is on the right foot. As the weight comes forward on to the left foot, the ball is thrown.

(Compare Plate 59.)

"Come to meet it"

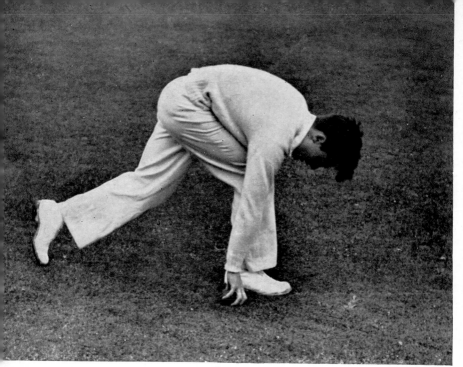

61

61.

Here the ball has passed the fielder who has had to chase it.
The fielder keeps the ball on his right side.

The ball is gathered with the right hand, *before* the fielder
turns round.

Don't try to pick the ball up too soon—you must overrun it.

Don't try to throw while you are still off balance. This
does *not* save time.

62

62.

The fielder has not been able to get two hands to this one, but has used the right foot to back up the hand. Even if the ball is not gathered cleanly, it will not reach the boundary.

Note that the eyes are on the ball.

63

64

65

63, 64.

Throwing cannot be taught—it must be learnt by practice.

These photographs illustrate the basic points.

Note (i) the transfer of weight from the right to the left foot as the throw is made ;

(ii) the follow through ;

(iii) the eyes fixed on the target.

65.

If the batsmen are stealing a quick single and the ball is moving slowly, the fielders near the wicket can save time by throwing underarm. The ball is gathered on the run with the right hand only and is thrown in the same movement. Safety here is sacrificed for speed.

Note that the eyes must be on the ball while it is being gathered. In the plate, the fielder, having gathered the ball safely, is now taking aim at the wicket.

" Throw to the top of the stumps "

WICKET-KEEPING

KEEPING wicket is perhaps the most tiring job in cricket, and to keep for a whole day without missing a catch or letting a bye is as much a feat of sustained effort and concentration as anything else. If you are, or are going to be, a wicket-keeper you must be prepared to work hard and not to relax. You will, or should be, judged not on what you have done, but on what you have failed to do. The taking of five catches in an innings does not necessarily indicate a good wicket-keeper, but the missing of five indicates a bad one. It follows that the first requirement for a good keeper is the power of concentration.

Concentration. Every ball which is bowled may reach the wicket-keeper, and you must therefore be sure that your hands are always ready to take the ball, whether you think that the batsman will hit it or not. If you relax this precaution for a moment during a long stand, you may miss a vital catch which would change the course of the game. Most bowlers are resigned to catches being missed in the field, but every bowler has a right to expect that chances at the wicket will be taken. You may be justly proud if bowlers have this confidence in you. The reward for wicket-keeping comes, not from the crowd who applaud one brilliant piece of work, but from the bowler who says, " I like having you as a wicket-keeper. I know you'll catch them."

Stumping. Every wicket-keeper may expect anything up to five chances of a catch to every one chance of stumping. It must therefore be your first concern to see that *every* ball is taken cleanly, and you must *avoid all tendency to snatch*, even if the batsman has left his ground. You will find also that you will miss more chances of stumping through failing to take the ball, than through being too slow in breaking the wicket. Further, never be afraid to stand back to fast bowling, if you think that you are likely to miss catches by standing up. When standing back, *stand well back*. The ball should be taken just after it has reached the highest point in its path. A " half and half " position merely makes things more difficult.

Style. All your movements must be free and loose. If your hands and arms are cramped or rigid, you will never keep well, and injuries to your fingers will be frequent. *Always get your hands to the ball.* Your pads are for protection only. There should be no second line of defence for wicket-keepers.

Avoid all flashiness. The quietest wicket-keeper is usually the best.

Taking the Ball. The theory of wicket-keeping is to keep the head as near as possible to, and the hands on, the line of the ball.

When you take up your stance, your head is low and your hands are near the ground. Unless the ball is outside the leg stump, or very wide on the off, you should maintain this position until the ball has pitched. As the ball rises, come up with it, keeping your hands on the same level as the ball. You will then find that the ball will be taken cleanly and that your hands will automatically " give " a little as you receive it. A downward movement of the hands just before taking the ball is always wrong. When you are keeping to slow bowling, the " give " of the hands is unnecessary, but you must still avoid snatching. The hands can start somewhat outside the line of the ball and sweep to the wicket, taking the ball *en route*. If the movement is smooth the ball can be taken cleanly, and time is saved in stumping.

When standing up, you have no time to move your hands if the ball is deflected by the bat. Therefore take the ball as near the bat as possible (but not in front of the wicket), so that this deflection will be small. A counsel of perfection is : outside the off stump, take the ball in the left hand ; outside the leg stump, in the right hand. This allows the maximum for deflection, but is beyond the scope of all but the most highly skilled wicket-keepers. Do not be disheartened if you miss a catch. Some catches at the wicket are impossible—the deflection is too great. If you would have taken the ball had the batsman not hit it, you have done all in your power.

Outside the Leg Stump. There is considerable difference of opinion among wicket-keepers as to how to take a ball outside the leg stump. Some maintain that they wait until they can judge the flight of the ball off the pitch, and then move across (quick-footed gentlemen these !). At least one believes in watching the ball from the normal position and shooting out the hands only. (You must be pretty good for this.) We feel that the best policy is to go across as soon as you see that the ball will be outside the batsman's legs. Go right across so that you have a clear view, and you may be able to sight it again—but we doubt it. If you are a wicket-keeper the ball will arrive in your hands, and if you aren't, it won't !

Injuries. If you damage your hands, whenever possible take a rest. Otherwise fear of hurting yourself may lead you into bad habits. If you have to play, protect the injured part carefully. A bruise can be covered with plasticine. An injured finger should be bound up with adhesive tape, and two fingers of the glove strapped together. But always remember, *the best protection against injury is to take the ball correctly.*

68

66, 67. Stance

The feet are apart, heels on ground.
The wicket-keeper is close to the wicket.
Note the general feeling of ease and balance so that free
movement is possible in any direction.

68. Wrong

The feet are together, heels off the ground.
The wicket is out of reach.
The position is cramped and uncomfortable so that no move-
ment can be made without first standing up.

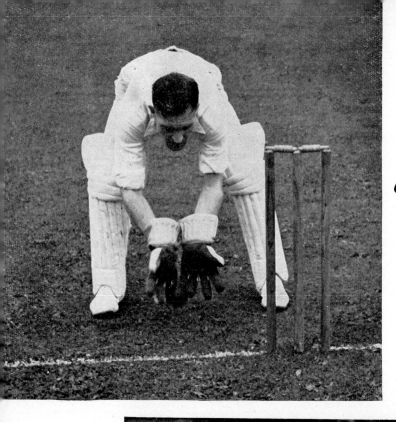

69

70

69. An Over-pitched One

Compare this plate with Plate 66.

The wicket-keeper has stayed " down " until the ball has pitched.

The fingers are pointing down.

Note that the legs are *not* used as a second line of defence, as this would cramp the movement of the hands and make it impossible to take the ball cleanly.

70.

As the ball rises, the wicket-keeper comes up with it.

The fingers are pointing down.

The elbows are away from the body, allowing free movement to the hands and arms.

"Legs are a nuisance in wicket-keeping"

71

72

73

"WHERE DO THE FINGERS POINT?"

71. A Bumper

Still coming up with the ball—right on the toes.
The fingers are still pointing down.
Note the free movement of the elbows.

72.

Here the fingers are pointing upward to take a very high
one. Owing to the angle from which the photograph is taken,
the face is hidden by the hands. The ball can in fact be clearly
sighted.

73. A Wide One

The feet have moved for the first time—right foot only,
across not back.
The fingers point sideways.
The left hand forms a cup under the ball.
Note the position of the head—eyes on the ball.

"Look after your hands. They do the work"

74. Outside the Leg Stump

Both feet have moved across.
The right foot is near the wicket, which is still within easy reach.
The wicket-keeper has stayed " down."

75. Run Out

The wicket is between the keeper and the fielder.
The ball is taken as near the stumps as possible.

76. Reward

Don't snatch !

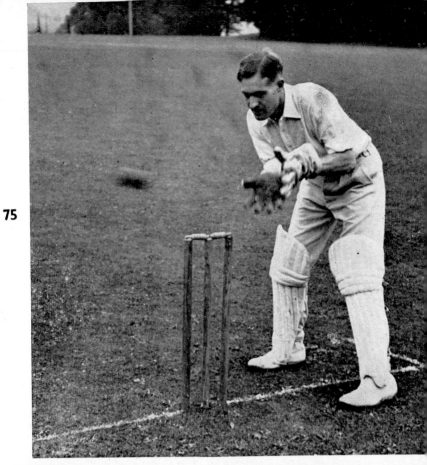

75

76

77

" A CONFESSION OF FAILURE "

77.
NEVER !

CONCLUSION

In the preceding pages we have tried to cover most of the technical side of a cricketer's art. We do not expect that every cricketer will agree with all we have written. We have found too much difficulty in reaching agreement ourselves for that ! We shall be satisfied if this book, by emphasising certain fundamental points and provoking discussion on others, helps the young (and perhaps also the not so young) players to improve their game.

We have said little on the strategy or tactics of cricket. This is not because we wish to belittle this aspect of the game, but because we feel that it is not susceptible to visual illustration and as such it would be out of place in a book of this type. For the same reason we have reduced the narrative to a minimum. Also because we firmly believe that the future of cricket always remains in the hands of youth, we have concentrated upon what we hope will prove to be an attractive form of presentation.

Finally we would remind our readers that cricket is a game and as such it should give pleasure to player and spectator alike. If we have in any way added to that pleasure our efforts will not have been in vain.